BEN BAILEY

THE MOODY COOK

AUSTIN MACAULEY PUBLISHERS®
LONDON · CAMBRIDGE · NEW YORK · SHARJAH

A CIP catalogue record for this title is available from the British Library.

ISBN 9781035895311 (Paperback)
ISBN 9781035895328 (Hardback)
ISBN 9781035895335 (ePub e-book)

www.austinmacauley.com

First Published 2026
Austin Macauley Publishers Ltd®
1 Canada Square
Canary Wharf
London
E14 5AA

I would like to dedicate the photography to my partner, Bo, and to my mother, Nicky, for being afraid of the kitchen and pushing me to start my cooking journey.

Table of Contents

About Me

Since I was a teenager, cooking has always played a big part in my life. It started out of necessity at the time but has become a passion later in my life. My mother was, and still is, a self-confessed abomination in the kitchen. She made a decision early on in her marriage to my father that she felt quite lightheaded every time she stepped near the cooker so for health reasons, she respectfully removed herself from these situations. My father wasn't much better, but he is from an era when men didn't cook. Well, unless you count cremating food on a barbeque as cooking.

I started cooking as a way of eating something that wasn't a ready meal or a frozen dinosaur shaped nugget. Not that I didn't love it. After all, I'm from the ready meal era, where anything can be created in under five minutes in the microwave.

In the early days, I wasn't very good or adventurous. A jacket potato here, a spag bowl there and to be frank, not much else in between.

This all changed at 23 when I packed up my little mini and set off on the adventure of a lifetime. Driving from the depths of Hertfordshire to Italy and spending six months discovering this beautiful country.

This was a trip I had been planning with great excitement, but also a few nerves. You see I had barely left the home counties up until this point, but I knew I wanted more and I knew there was so much more in the world to explore.

It was an instant love affair. Not just with food but also the people, the architecture, the atmosphere, the weather…The list goes on and on.

From the majestic basil lined hills of the Ligurian coast, to the rugged landscape of Tuscany and beyond, it was like nothing I had ever experienced before.

This was where my love affair, and indeed my skill for cooking, was really formed.

Between the Campari induced evenings I spent a lot of my time learning about the different cuisines, difference recipes and. of course, the different techniques from each region.

The richness of a slow cooked ragu from the north to the lightness of lemon infused pasta from the hedonistic lemons of the Amalfi coast, the flavours were as complex as their surroundings and its people and it's safe to say, I was forever changed in the best possible way.

Over a decade later, my repertoire has definitely broadened but my foundation for cooking and creating recipes is still very much linked to those skills I learnt throughout Italy.

For example, the wonderful sofrito is a foundation of most recipes I cook and will continue to be so for many years to come.

Over the years, I have been thinking about how my mood plays a key part in the food I crave as well as what I cook. Especially in these troubled times where food has become such a pivotal part of people's life, when so much else has been denied to us.

That is where this cookbook comes from. A book dedicated to recipes based on people's mood and life events.

Because what we want to eat when we have had a bad day in the office, may be a delicious, slow cooked beef pie, but let's face it, you have no mental capacity to spend hours in the kitchen.

When You Just Need Fuel

This mood is not dictated by weather, time of the year or day of the week. It is really specific to each and every one of us.

Of course, when it's cold outside you just want fuel, but there are so many more occasions where nothing else will do but a big hearty plate or bowl of something warming.

The big break up, the dreaded winter flu, when life feels just too much, the list goes on and on.

I am no psychologist, but I know that in these moments when we are not at our best we crave something that will fill us, comfort us and make us sing from the inside.

Whether you're sat at a grand dining table, by a roaring fire or in your cute London flat, the feeling is generally the same.

What does vary is the number of people you are cooking for, but don't fear if you are living your best life in a bijou Battersea flat and the recipe says for four.

That's what freezers or lunch/dinner the next day is for. Just think how satisfying it is going to be knowing that you have dinner sorted for the next few days and that it is going to contribute to those bright feelings that only fuel food can do.

Life can be bleak sometimes but the food you cook and eat doesn't have to be and these recipes will certainly prove that.

Cold And Flu And No Idea What To Do: This Calls For My Take On Jewish Penicillin

SERVES: 4 PREP TIME: 5 MINUTES COOK TIME: 30 MINUTES

This is going to sound controversial, but I have never been a big fan of a traditional chicken soup in the traditional broth form. It may be that I have never had a good one or never mastered the stock, but to me, it's not something I would reach for at any time of the year.

I can't deny its healing benefits and whenever I have had a cold or flu and it has been made for me, the recovery time is always much faster.

When we are sick, we automatically reach for simple food, usually in the form of a takeaway or ready meal, because the sheer thought of cooking is enough to keep you in bed for an extra few days.

But that's what partners, parents and best friends are for. If you're feeling rotten and can't face standing over the hob, rope those loved ones in to make you this super simple, but super powerful supper.

This recipe is my take on an Italian Christmas classic, usually had as the first of many courses on the big day and is referred to lovingly as tortellini in brodo.

Not that any self-respecting Italian would use shop bought tortellini, but you're sick and this is the time you need simplicity in your life, so I think we will be forgiven.

Happy recovery! I promise this will do the trick.

INGREDIENTS

250g bag of tortellini

1L chicken stock, a cube or gel is fine

1 banana shallot, roughly chopped

Handful flat leaf parsley, roughly chopped

2 cloves garlic, minced

1 tsp dried oregano

Olive oil

Salt and pepper

Parmesan to serve

INSTRUCTIONS

In a large saucepan, heat some olive oil over a medium heat and add your chopped banana shallot. This is the base of your delicious and nourishing broth so cook it nice and slow for about 5 minutes, stirring occasionally. The onions are ready when they have softened and that bright pink becomes translucent.

After this point, add your garlic and oregano and cook for a few minutes, just enough to release the aromas but not enough to colour or burn.

Now pour in your pre prepared chicken stock and bring to the boil. Once boiled, reduce to a simmer and add your tortellini, cooking to the packet instructions.

When the tortellini is cooked, throw in the fresh parsley, give it all a stir, along with a grinding of salt and pepper and taste for seasoning. Go easy on the salt to begin with as the stock may be salty and keep adding and tasting, until it is to your taste.

Finally add as much grated parmesan as you can handle, believe me it can take a lot!

Enjoy in a bowl, on the sofa, under the blanket and feel the miracle of this delicious broth heal you.

No Energy For Anything Weeks: Who Says You Can't Have Mash For Dinner?

SERVES: 4 PREP TIME: 15 MINUTES COOK TIME: 30 MINUTES

I am not going to sit here and pretend like this is the type of meal you should eat every day or is going to positively impact those love handles, although if you want to eat this every day, I say you do you and who cares.

But if your doctor asks, I didn't say that!

What this recipe is great for though is those weeks where you don't have any energy for anything. Whether that's due to the weather, workloads, kids playing up or just an endless to do list.

This may strike you as strange as it's not the quickest recipe I have ever created, but all the elements require very little of your, what I call, standing up time. This means you can create something so comforting, so delicious and exactly what you need on days when the world just feels too much, with minimal effort.

The reason I came up with this recipe was actually quite random as I was trying to find something to go with the Swedish meatballs my partner was making for our Eurovision night.

No, we are not that committed to the Eurovision cause but he is Swedish, so it is an obligatory event every year in our household!

I knew I wanted something potato based but I wasn't feeling plain old, boiled potatoes and chips were not an option. If you are a true Swede, this is a no-go outside of an Ikea canteen and even then, it isn't really accepted.

So then I thought mash but not just any mash, my creamy, baked, parmesan crusted mash. It was a real hit and works with pretty much anything.

I mean, has anyone ever said you can't have mash with that?

INGREDIENTS

5 potatoes, peeled and chopped into rough cubes	50g Grated parmesan, or thereabouts
125g mascarpone	50g Breadcrumbs, or thereabouts
1 tbsp milk	Salt and pepper

INSTRUCTIONS

Heat the oven to 180 degrees Celsius (fan) and place your potatoes in a pan of cold water, bringing them to the boil.

Boil the potatoes for about 15 minutes or until a knife slides through easily.

Transfer the potatoes to a large bowl and add the mascarpone and milk and mash together until smooth.

Once your mash is celestially smooth, season generously with salt and pepper and transfer to a baking dish.

Top the mash with enough Parmesan and breadcrumbs to cover the surface and bake in the oven for about 30 minutes, until the top is crispy and golden.

This can be eaten on its own in front of the TV if you are feeling really gluttonous or serve them with meatballs in a Swedish sauce with green beans like I did.

Either way, it will be delicious!

It's Been A Long Winter: Harissa All The Way

SERVES: 4 PREP TIME: 10 MINUTES COOK TIME: 30 MINUTES

We have all felt it, by the time we get to March, the winter feels like it has lasted a lifetime and we are all over the Hunters, the Barbour jackets and being constantly wet. What starts off as a scene from an old Dickens tale, curled up by a roaring fire in the depths of winter, by this point in the year, significantly loses its charm.

This is when you need a recipe like this. It's hearty, it's vibrant, it's flavourful and it packs the punch you need to get you through to when the sun reappears again.

It's certainly not elegant food but that is very much part of its charm. Imagine a layer of spicy mince, topped with crispy roast potatoes and that final bite of salty feta, mixed with the freshness of the fresh herbs.

I hate to say it, but it all builds up to an explosion in your mouth and will definitely fight away those winter blues.

INGREDIENTS

600g potatoes, chopped into small wedges

1 red onion, roughly hopped

1 clove garlic, finely chopped

500g beef mince

4 tsp rose harissa paste

1 tbsp dried oregano

100g feta, crumbled

400g can tinned tomatoes

Handful of fresh parsley and coriander, roughly chopped

Olive oil for cooking

Salt and pepper

INSTRUCTIONS

Pre heat the oven to 180 degrees Celsius. Pop your potatoes into a roasting dish. Drizzle with olive oil, salt and pepper. Mix together and pop in the oven for about 30 minutes, until golden and crispy.

Meanwhile, crack on with your mince…

Heat some olive oil in a pan on a medium heat and cook your onions for about 5 minutes, until they are lovely and soft. Make sure to stir regularly so they don't catch.

Next add your garlic and oregano, cooking for a few minutes to release their flavour, before whacking up the heat to high and browning the mince, mixing the delicious onions into the meat.

Once the mince is browned all over, season with a little salt and pepper, then add your tomatoes, water and harissa paste. Bring to the boil, stir and then reduce to a simmer for about 20 minutes, stirring occasionally.

Remove your potatoes from the oven, top with the mince and scatter the dish with the crumbled feta. Switch the oven to a medium grill and pop the dish under the grill for about 5 minutes, until it's browned on the edges and the feta begins to colour.

Remove from the oven and scatter with a hedonistic amount of your parsley and coriander and dig in! Enjoy.

The Hangover Cure: The Glorious Grain Of Rice

SERVES: 4 PREP TIME: 5 MINUTES COOK TIME: 10 MINUTES

We have all been there, the morning after the night before. The impromptu after work drink with friends, that ended up in that late night establishment you swore at the beginning of the night you would never frequent again.

Now it's morning. Your head is pounding and you are full of regret. But boy was it a good night! So don't be hard on yourself. Life is too short to regret these moments.

You are already contemplating food that will cure you though. Will it be that cheesy, salty pizza or that processed but delicious burger from that fast food chain we all know and love?

Well, I have an unconventional idea, something I know may send your brain into an anaphylactic shock, but why don't you cook something up?

Novel idea, and from first-hand experience, I know how this is the last thing you want to do when you are feeling like this. But I am not talking about some cordon bleu masterpiece, but rather a firm takeaway favourite, egg fried rice.

So simple to make, it will take less time than it will take for you to order it and for it to be delivered from that charming local restaurant. I find a bit of monotonous stirring really helps take your mind away from how the effects of the night before are making me feel.

I promise you won't regret it. You will feel great after and don't worry if you don't have any cooked and cooled rice to hand, use a packet of microwave rice. It works just as well. Speedy recovery my fellow party animals.

INGREDIENTS

250g cooked and cooled rice	1 ½ tsp Chinese five spice
1 large yellow onion, finely chopped	1 tbsp sweet chili sauce or runny honey
1tbsp garlic puree (from a tube)	2 tbsp soy sauce
3 large eggs	Olive oil
50g frozen peas	Salt and pepper

INSTRUCTIONS

The humble grain of rice has never tasted so good!

Heat some oil in a pan under a low heat, whisk together your eggs and add to the pan, stirring regularly, until you have lightly cooked scrambled eggs. Remove to a plate and set aside.

Add some more oil to a pan, turn the heat up to medium and add your chopped onion, along with a pinch of salt.

Cook for about 5 minutes, until soft.

Throw in the garlic and Chinese five spice, cook for about 1 minute to release the garlic flavour and cook out the spice, before popping the cooked rice in and mixing everything together

Add your peas, an additional sprinkle of five spice, soy sauce, sweet chili sauce and a grinding of pepper and cook together until the peas are cooked and the rice is re-heated, about 5 minutes.

Finally throw the egg back in, give it a stir and taste for seasoning. You may need more soy sauce if it tastes a little bland.

Enjoying this in front of the TV is, in my opinion, obligatory.

Enjoy your Friday night guys and hope this helps cure anyone else feeling ever so slightly delicate today.

I’m Going Out With The Boys And Need To Line My Stomach: Swedish Hot Dog It Is

SERVES: 2 TO 6 PREP TIME: 5 MINUTES COOK TIME: 10 MINUTES

Before I met my partner, I thought a hot dog was just a frankfurter in a bun, topped with ketchup, mustard and potentially some grilled onions.

Not that there is anything wrong with this, quite the opposite. These delectable pink beauties conjure up fond memories of childhood birthday parties and suppers in the garden.

But let me tell you, these Swedish versions are a complete game changer.

You may be thinking why my partner is relevant to this story. Even if you are not, I shall tell you anyway. He is Swedish. He is also the one who introduced this version of a hot dog to me on my first trip to Stockholm and I became instantly obsessed, so much so, in the 3 days I was there, I had one every day!

Our Scandinavian friends have brought us many things like Abba, Ikea and Vikings but if I am being honest, I have never thought about them as a culinary marvel but I have really enjoyed exploring their cuisine.

These hot dogs are familiar in the sense they are a frankfurter in a bun, there is ketchup and mustard involved, but they are topped with a form of prawn cocktail.

I know, to a non-Scandinavian, this sounds barmy, but please trust me, it is a match made in heaven and perfect when you need a quick bite to line your stomach for plenty of livations with your mates.

INGREDIENTS

- Hotdog sausages, one for each person
- Hotdog buns, again one for each person
- 1 tub of ready-made prawn cocktail
- Crispy onions
- Ketchup and mustard

INSTRUCTIONS

Boil or grill your frankfurter sausages according to the packet instructions and whilst they are cooking, warm your hotdog buns in a 180 degrees oven for about 5 minutes.

All that's left to do is assemble and this is quite important. If you divert from this method in any way, you will end up with a soggy mess. However, if you follow my instructions perfectly, you are in for a treat and luckily, the instructions aren't complicated.

Place your cooked hotdog into your bun, top with a squirt of mustard and ketchup, a thin line the full length of the hot dog, and finally top this with a few tablespoons of your prawn cocktail mixture and a generous sprinkle of crispy onions.

Repeat this until you have the amount of hotdogs you would like and if you are feeling extra fancy, top with some fresh dill.

These are best enjoyed with a glass of cold beer on a hot summer's day, but to be honest, they are great any time of the year or day for that matter.

When The World Looks Bleak !

We all have those days, weeks or months when things just aren't going our way and the world looks bleak.

There are many reasons for this, a bad time at work, failed relationship, loss of a loved one, children not playing ball, the list goes on and on. Since the pandemic, we know how important it is to combat these moments and help in any way we can to get to better times.

These are all inevitable moments that will happen in one way or another throughout our lives, but there are many things you can do to help you get through them. Some people meditate, some people do yoga and hell some people even work out. I do none of these things. I eat!

I believe that the gloriousness of food has the ability to impact our lives for the better and the philosophy behind this book is cooking based on your mood.

A famous Lao Tzu's quote was "to conquer others is to have power, to conquer yourself is to know the way". I fundamentally believe this, and food will help you find the way to brighter days.

When you are in this phase of your life, you don't have the mental space to spend hours in the kitchen and to be creative and add flair. Equally, you don't want to reach for your favourite takeaway menu every night, as easy as that may be.

In this section, you will find many delicious recipes that are perfect for when you are not feeling your best. These recipes are simple, effective and packed full of flavour.

They are just the recipes to bring you out of your slump.

Feed The Soul With Creamy Pasta: Tortellini In A Cream Sauce

SERVES: 6 PREP TIME: 5 MINUTES COOK TIME: 10 MINUTES

What could be more comforting than the smell of fresh filled pasta cooking away and then layer that with the delicate creaminess of crème fraiche. If the smell doesn't transfix you, then the taste certainly will.

This recipe will take away those feelings of bleakness in the dark depths of the winter and the evergreen majestic basil leaves will make you think of brighter times ahead.

This recipe came to me on one of those rainy nights when I couldn't sleep and all I could think about was what I was going to have for dinner that very evening.

Knowing I would be tired, cold and probably a little blue, it needed to be simple for sure. Above all though I had a craving for something creamy.

My favourite dish of all time is a carbonara and this is my homage to that, in a much lighter way.

INGREDIENTS

300g tortellini

1 red onion, finely chopped

2 cloves garlic, finely chopped

200ml low fat creme fraiche

50g grated Parmesan

Handful frozen peas

Olive oil

Salt and pepper

INSTRUCTIONS

Heat some oil in a large nonstick pan, over a medium heat and add your onion. Cook for about 5 minutes, until lovely and soft.

Add your garlic and cook for a few minutes before adding the creme fraiche. Let this cook down on a gentle heat for about 5 minutes.

Whilst your sauce is cooking, bring a large saucepan of water to the boil and add your tortellini and frozen peas, cooking according to the packet instructions.

When the tortellini and peas are cooked, transfer them to the sauce, along with a little pasta cooking water.

Combine everything, throw in your parmesan and season with a little salt and pepper as needed.

The Big Breakup: Peanut Butter Is The Only Cure

SERVES: 4 PREP TIME: 5 MINUTES COOK TIME: 20 MINUTES

Something we have all experienced, and often more frequently in your early 20s than your 30s, but the beauty of breakups in your early 20s is that your waistline can afford the ice cream and a whole tub of peanut butter with a spoon in bed.

Unfortunately, the same can't be said when you're in your 30s or 40s. Not only do you have to contend with the heartbreak of losing a more serious relationship, but you can't even console yourself with those delicious comfort foods you used to.

Well, you can but you won't enjoy the crash diet you have to go on when you come to your senses.

What you can do is have that silky, smoothness that only peanut butter can give you, but in a protein packed chicken curry.

Doesn't that sound like a great way to sooth a breakup and you'll feel a lot less guilty when trying to lick the remains out of the jar, not to mention the loss of you're dignity.

INGREDIENTS

4 chicken thighs, chopped into bite-sized chunks	1 tsp red pepper flakes
1 onion, roughly chopped	Juice of one lime
300ml chicken stock (from a cube)	1 tsp soy sauce
1 heaped tbsp smooth peanut butter	Handful fresh coriander, roughly chopped
1 heaped tbsp ground coriander	Olive oil
1 tsp ground cumin	Salt and pepper

INSTRUCTIONS

Season your chicken chunks with a good amount of salt and pepper. I would say about a teaspoon of each as under seasoned meat is not the one!

Heat some oil in a large pan, over a medium heat and brown the chicken for a few minutes.

Once the chicken is browned all over, add the onions to the pan and cook for about 5 minutes until softened. Clamping on a lid helps with this.

Add the ground coriander, cumin and red pepper flakes. Cook for a few minutes, to cook out the spices. To this pan of spicy goodness, add the peanut butter, chicken stock, lime juice and soy sauce.

Bring to a simmer, clamp on a lid and simmer for 8 to 10 minutes until the chicken is cooked. Stir every so often so the sauce doesn't catch on the bottom of the pan.

Finally, throw on some freshly chopped coriander and serve with some microwave rice. Hope this helps mend the broken heart!

Long Day In The Office: A Hug In A Bowl Tomato Soup

SERVES: 4 PREP TIME: 10 MINUTES COOK TIME: 30 MINUTES

When I think of tomato soup, it always conjures up memories of my travels to Italy and those delectable, sweet, red morsels foraged from the foothills of Mount Vesuvius.

The cold depths of Hertfordshire or the dusty streets of London don't quite have the same ring to it, but thanks to the wonders of importation, we can now get delicious Italian tomatoes in tin form. Mutti is a brand that I have just discovered and, whilst a little pricey, they are the best tinned tomatoes on the market, and you can pick them up from most supermarkets now.

At Christmas, we all want to counteract the mountain of mince pies and treats we have all consumed in December.

However, that doesn't mean we have to compromise on flavour and this rich tomato soup is so celestial in taste you wouldn't believe it was actually good for you.

The other beauty of this recipe is how simple it is to make, and it uses ingredients that everyone will have in their cupboards. Perfect for a mid-week family meal or a simple dinner for when friends pop round at the last minute.

INGREDIENTS

2 400g cans of chopped tomatoes	1 tbsp dried oregano
2 fat garlic cloves, roughly chopped	1 tsp fresh rosemary
1 large yellow onion (red will also be fine)	1 tsp fresh or dried thyme
1 tbsp tomato puree	Olive oil
500ml chicken or veg stock from a cube	Salt and pepper

INSTRUCTIONS

Heat a large saucepan over a medium heat with some olive oil and while this heats up, chop your onion. The onion doesn't have to be fine as you will be blitzing the soup later. Add the onion to the pan with a pinch of salt and sweat down for about 5 minutes, until they have softened.

Once the onions have softened, add the garlic and allow the lovely, garlicky aromas to release for about a minute before adding the tomato puree.

Add the oregano, rosemary and thyme to the tomatoey onions and cook for a few minutes to get rid of that raw tomato flavour.

Once you have achieved this, add the tinned tomatoes, stock, salt and pepper (to taste). Stir everything well and bring to the boil.

Reduce the heat to a simmer and cook the soup for about 15 minutes, stirring occasionally.

Transfer the soup to a blender or use a stick blender and blend until completely smooth. Then transfer back to the pan, taste and add salt and pepper as needed.

Enjoy with a slice of fresh rye bread and feel smug about how healthy you have been.

Tips: If you don't have fresh rosemary and thyme, use the same amount of dried and it will taste just great.

If you aren't using the sweet Mutti tomatoes, no problem, but add a pinch of sugar and that will counteract the slight bitterness.

Up For Something New: A Real Turkish Delight

SERVES: 4 PREP TIME: 10 MINUTES COOK TIME: 25 MINUTES

Last year, I decided to take myself away from my beloved Italian cuisine and test recipes properly from other areas of the globe. Don't get me wrong; I will always have a real love affair with Italian food, the culture and way of life from my time living there many years ago, but there are so many other flavours to explore, and I am ready to explore all of them, in all their spectacular glory.

Shakshuka is a prime example of this.

For me, food is about the feelings and memories it evokes and although I have no experience of trying this in the midst of an Istanbul souk, the feeling it evokes for me is one of ultimate comfort, warming and just wow.

I remember the first time I tried this. It was in a well-known high street chain in west London on a lovely Sunday afternoon, after a long walk along the riverbanks of Chiswick. As always, when I am doing any form of exercise, my thoughts quickly turned to food and my other half told me of this great little bistro he had been to before.

Obviously, I didn't need any persuading and as I perused the menu, my eyes were immediately drawn to the shakshuka. Not usually something I would go for, to be honest, but the descriptions of those exotic flavours were calling my name.

The result: complete and utter culinary pleasure. I obviously had to go straight home and work out how to re-create this delicious dish myself.

INGREDIENTS

2 400g tinned chopped tomatoes

1 red chilli, finely chopped

1 large red onion, finely chopped

3 garlic cloves, finely chopped

1 red pepper, cut into slices

1 tsp Aleppo pepper (if you have it)

1 tsp caster sugar

4 large eggs

Handful of fresh coriander, chopped

Olive oil

Salt and pepper

INSTRUCTIONS

Heat some oil in a large, shallow frying pan or casserole dish over a medium heat and once the oil has heated up, add the onions and about ½ tsp salt to draw out the moisture.

Cook for 5 to 8 minutes stirring regularly until the onions have softened and released their oniony flavour.

Once this has happened, add your garlic, chilli and red pepper, cooking for a few minutes to cook out the raw garlic and soften the pepper slightly.

How fabulous does your kitchen smell now? Pop in your tinned tomatoes, sugar, Aleppo pepper, coriander stalks and season with a little salt and pepper. Bring this to the boil and then reduce to a gentle simmer for about 10 minutes, to let the flavours blend together.

Time to add the eggs. Make 4 indentations in the sauce and crack an egg into each of them, seasoning just the top of the egg with a little salt and pepper.

Make sure the heat is on low, clamp on a lid and cook for around 6 minutes or until your eggs are set.

Finally throw on the fresh coriander leaves in a Jackson Pollock fashion and dig in with a slice of toasted, crunchy sourdough.

This is great hangover food. The spice and fresh herbs help wash away the pain.

Note: If you don't have a fresh chilli, 1 tsp of dried chilli flakes will do the job as well.

Worried About Money, Cheap Eats

Why is it always the way that there seems to be more money going out than coming in, well hopefully not always. But we all have those times in our lives where we feel like we are constantly chasing our tales when it comes to finance.

These can be incredibly stressful times when eating healthily isn't really a priority. It's all about fuelling yourself and your loved ones as cheaply as possible.

In these times, it can be so easy to reach for that bag of frozen chicken dippers and chips and, as we all know, they will fill that void and if we are really honest, they taste pretty good and they are cheap. Although maybe it's more nostalgia than flavour that makes them taste so good.

This section is here to show you that you don't have to delve into the depths of the frozen section at the supermarket. You can create delicious, nutritious and sometimes a little naughty meals without a cardiac from the bank manager.

From the versatility flavour soakers that are the humble lentil, to the juiciness and cost efficiency of the chicken thigh.

The key generally lies in the flavourings and your dried spices, all of which can make even the cheapest of ingredients taste divine.

Stressed Out By All the Leftovers: Chicken Pie Is The Only Way To Go

SERVES: 6 PREP TIME: 10 MINUTES COOK TIME: 30 MINUTES

It's the end of the week and you have spent the majority of your week cooking. That is great, by the way, and you should be very proud, but that also means that you are overrun with leftovers.

There's the partially eaten chicken, that one lonely onion and those fresh herbs that are very nearly past their best. Let's face it, with the price of fresh herbs these days, you can't be throwing them away.

Good news is that you have all the basics for a delicious, creamy and velvety chicken pie.

The perfect Sunday recipe and it's extremely versatile, with lots of adaptable ingredients. You shouldn't even have to run to the shops.

For example, swap the pastry topping for mash with the leftover potatoes, or if you don't have crème fraîche, swap it for ricotta, double cream or even cream cheese.

Enjoy this one and if you can get your kids or family members to help with the preparations, even more sofa time for you.

Happy Sunday all!

INGREDIENTS

500g leftover chicken	2 cloves garlic, finely chopped
2 tbsp plain flour	1 tsp each of fresh thyme and rosemary, chopped
500ml chicken stock (from a cube)	1 large knob butter
1 sheet of all butter puff pastry	1 egg, lightly beaten
Leftover veg, I had carrots and peas	Salt and pepper
2 tbsp crème fraiche	1 large onion, roughly chopped
1 tsp Dijon mustard	

INSTRUCTIONS

Heat some olive oil in a large pan and fry the onions for about 5 minutes until translucent.

Add the garlic and cook for a further minute to soften the garlic slightly, before adding the butter.

Stir in the flour and cook for a couple of minutes. This stage is important as you want the flour to cook slightly and be rid of the raw flour taste in the finished dish.

Once the flour has turned a nutty brown, start to add the stock, a little at a time, and whisking between each addition to avoid lumps.

Once all the stock has been added, bring to the boil and let it simmer on a medium heat for 5 minutes until the sauce has thickened slightly.

Add the chicken, vegetables, rosemary, thyme, Dijon mustard and crème fraiche. Give everything a stir and season to taste, the stock will be quite salty so go easy on the salt.

Transfer to an oven proof dish and top the filling with the sheet of puff pastry.

Brush the top of the pastry with some beaten egg, this will make it majestically brown!

Bake in the oven at 180 Celsius (fan) for about 30 minutes. Once the pastry is puffed and browned, it is ready to serve.

Post Holiday Blues: The Only Cure Is To Re-Live It Through The Food!

SERVES: 12 cheese balls   PREP TIME: 5 MINUTES   COOK TIME: 15 MINUTES

I'm sure we are all the same in this, but the holiday blues are the worst, aren't they?

It wasn't so bad as a child because coming back from two weeks away in Portugal still meant there were nearly six weeks left of the summer holidays. Long days out with friends from sunrise to sunset, without a care in the world.

In fact, in those days, all you had to worry about was to be home in time for dinner and if mum had washed your favourite t-shirt, which, let's face it, she never had when you wanted it.

As an adult, returning from holiday means a week's worth of washing, finding out no one has actioned anything on your handover notes, landing on your delayed flight back to Luton at midnight and then getting up at 6 a.m. for a rude awakening to your first day back at work.

Don't get me wrong; there are so many positives to being an adult, and I love it! There is the freedom to do what you want, you have your own money and that overwhelming sense of superiority against the younger generation.

Nevertheless, coming back from a holiday is the hard part of being an adult.

With this in mind, my next recipe is about bringing those fond holiday memories back.

I won't say the original name for this recipe but think Brazilian cheese balls, a food I have adored ever since my father married my lovely Brazilian stepmother many years ago and one I start thinking about when I am at the airport in London on my way to Brazil.

This is my take on them and I hope they help wash away your holiday blues!

INGREDIENTS

227ml milk	2 large eggs
113ml vegetable oil	185g grated parmesan
284ml tapioca flour (available on Amazon)	1 tsp course sea salt

INSTRUCTIONS

Pour the milk, oil and salt into a medium saucepan and heat on a medium heat until it just comes to the boil.

Add the tapioca flour to the pan and mix until combined.

Transfer the mixture to an electric mixer and mix on medium for a few minutes until the mixture has softened and cooled slightly.

Still on medium speed, add the eggs one at a time, making sure each egg is incorporated before adding the next.

Add the Parmesan and beat in by hand.

Spray a muffin tin with non-stick spray or rub some vegetable oil into each of the cavities with some kitchen roll and drop about 1 tbsp rounds of the mixture into each of the cavities.

Bake in the oven at 180 degrees Celsius (fan) for 15 minutes, until they are lightly golden and have risen beautifully.

Best eaten warm straight from the oven, with cream cheese or on their own!

Needing Life's Little Comforts: My Take On My Nans Shepherd's Pie

SERVES: 6 PREP TIME: 10 MINUTES COOK TIME: 80 MINUTES

In difficult times, we all edge towards feelings, moments and foods that make us feel safe and happy. Let's face it, over the past few years we are all deserving of a little comfort.

Food has always been used as a barm in troubled times and we all have that recipe or favourite take out that takes us back to a time of comfort and happiness.

For me, it's the humble yet satisfying shepherd's pie. It's something my Nan used to make every time we went to visit and evokes wonderful memories.

Now that she is gone, every time I make it, I think of her and the wonderful memories of those summers, winters, springs. To be honest anytime of the year moments.

The whole family sat around the dining table, laughing, joking, drinking and catching up on life.

When I make this dish, it instantly puts a smile on my face. From the slow and steady stirring of the onions to the intense browning of the lamb mince, it fills me with a sense of calm and makes me feel like I can tackle any of life's issues.

I hope it does the same for all of you.

INGREDIENTS

1kg lamb mince	1tsp dried oregano
1 large onion	500ml beef stock (from a cube)
2 carrots	1 tbsp gravy granules
1 stick celery	1kg potatoes, peeled and chopped into chunks
3 cloves garlic, peeled	200g butter
1 sprig fresh rosemary, finely chopped	Olive oil
1 tbsp milk	Salt & pepper

INSTRUCTIONS

Heat some oil over a medium heat in a shallow pan and blitz your carrot, onion, celery and garlic in a food processor until finely chopped.

Add this mixture to the pan with a pinch of salt and pepper and cook for about 10 minutes until soft, not forgetting to stir occasionally.

Next add your lamb mince and move around the pan until it's browned all over. At this point, add the rosemary, oregano and beef stock, before reducing the heat to low and clamping on a lid.

Simmer your sauce gently for about 15 minutes, until the liquid has reduced a little. While you wait for this to happen, fill a large pot with water and pop on the heat to boil.

When your sauce has reduced, add the gravy granulates. Stir

and set aside to cool.

Add your chopped potatoes to the pan of boiling water, along with some salt. Cook the potatoes for about 20 minutes. The potatoes are ready when a knife goes through them easily and check them after 15 minutes, just in case.

Drain the potatoes and pop them back in the pot with the butter, milk, 1/2 tsp salt and a grinding of pepper. Mash everything with a potato masher until velvety and smooth.

Now to layer! Get a large baking dish out, start by pouring the lamb mixture into the dish, then top with the mash. Smooth the mash all over with a spatula so it covers the top and is smooth.

Bake in a pre-heated 180 degrees Celsius oven for about 40 minutes, or until the top is crispy and the sauce underneath is bubbling away.

Serve simply with some boiled peas and a scattering of fresh parsley if you have it. Unbeatable comfort food.

It's Not Treat Day But I Can't Face Another Salad: It's Got To Be Chicken Korma

SERVES: 4 PREP TIME: 5 MINUTES COOK TIME: 15 MINUTES

Why is it the first few days of the week you can eat healthily without even thinking about it and you feel incredibly smug, like what's the problem, this healthy eating malarkey is a piece of cake.

Then it gets to day five and the thought of yet another salad or bowl of quinoa is enough to send you into a mythological fury type of rage.

No matter how much you pretend, you know exactly what I mean.

The good news is, there are so many ways to be healthy and it doesn't have to involve bland, flavourless lean meat and vegetables.

I know what you are thinking, how can a chicken korma be healthy? I am telling you, it really can!

The typical takeaway version is laden with cream, but my version still has that same velvety creaminess, but without the excess calories.

By simply substituting the cream with coconut milk, you still get the same great, creamy flavour. But in a form that your personal trainer would be proud of.

Happy non-treat day! Not that you would know it wasn't, that is.

INGREDIENTS

2 chicken thighs, chopped into cubes	Handful fresh coriander, roughly chopped
2 tbsp korma paste	Olive oil
1 tsp ground coriander	Salt and pepper
1 tsp ground cumin	1 tsp ginger, garlic paste (from a jar)
1 400ml can coconut milk	1 tsp soy sauce
1 onion, roughly chopped	Handful frozen peas

INSTRUCTIONS

Heat some oil on a medium heat, in a medium-sized saucepan and add the chicken.

Cook for 5-7 minutes until cooked through, season with salt and pepper and set to one side on a plate.

Add your onion to the chicken juices in the pan and cook with a little salt for about 5 minutes, until soft. Follow this with the ginger and garlic paste and the korma paste, cooking out for a few minutes.

Add your dried spices, cooking for a minute and then add the coconut milk, soy sauce and reserved chicken.

Once the sauce comes to a gentle bubble, add the frozen peas and cook for a few minutes until they are cooked.

Finally throw over the fresh coriander and serve nice and simple with any microwave rice you fancy.

Last Week Before Payday: The Cheapness And Versatility Of Lentils

SERVES: 6 PREP TIME: 10 MINUTES COOK TIME: 30 MINUTES

It's that time of the month. Payday is five days away. The penny jar has already been raided, and whilst you promised yourself you wouldn't go out for those Thursday night drinks, you did. Oh, and guess what? You had one too many drinks and got a little generous.

What's done is done and you may be poor, but you have some great memories. The issue now is: What are you going to do about food for the next five days?

Let's be honest; it has to be delicious or you will reach for the takeaway menu, but it has to be, above all, cheap.

Now that is where the humble lentil comes into play. Although if you spoke to my mother, she would disagree. To her, the lentil is an abomination.

Don't ask me why. She tells me it's because she is from a time before fancy ingredients and doesn't listen to my argument that lentils outdate the Aztecs.

Like most people of her generation, she is stuck in her ways.

I urge you not to listen as the sweet, vibrant, hedonistic scent and taste of a good dhal is enough to transport you to a place you will never want to leave.

It's filling, it's delicious and above all, it's cheap, so it will get you through those last few days before payday and you won't even feel like you have had to go without. It's a real win-win!

INGREDIENTS

220g green lentils

1 tbsp ginger, garlic paste (shop bought)

1 large onion, roughly chopped

1 tsp curry powder

1 tsp turmeric

1 tbsp garam masala

½ tsp fennel seeds

1 400g can chopped tomatoes

1 400g can coconut milk

600ml vegetable stock (from a cube)

Olive Oil

Salt and pepper

INSTRUCTIONS

Heat some oil in a large saucepan, over a medium heat and add your onions with a little salt. Cook until soft, stirring occasionally for about 5 minutes.

Add your ginger, garlic paste, along with the fennel seeds and cook for a further minute until beautifully fragrant.

Add your remaining dried spices, cook out for a minute and then add your lentils, followed by the coconut milk, tomatoes and stock.

Season with a little salt and bring everything to the boil. Reduce to a simmer and simmer for about 30 minutes.

You want the dhal to be quite thick so if it's not, cook for a little longer.

Serve with your favourite flatbread or rice or both and a scattering of fresh coriander if you have any. What a delicious way to count the pennies!

Feeling Nostalgic Looking Through Old Photos: The Only Thing More Nostalgic Is Lasagne

SERVES: 6 PREP TIME: 10 MINUTES COOK TIME: 90 MINUTES

I don't know if it's just me, but the older I get, the more nostalgic I feel. I find myself time and time again looking at something, stumbling across some old photos and being instantly taken back to those sublime times.

These are those happy times of the day when you catch a break from chores, emails, meetings, the list goes on and on.

Occasionally, you have those moments and the memories aren't so good, but for the sake of this recipe, we will focus on the good memories.

These occasions, more often than not, involve food in some shape or form and the food we ate in those moments fills us with a huge sense of joy and comfort.

In these moments, we need a recipe that will bring us that same feeling in the present day.

That's where my lasagne is perfectly placed. It's not traditionally Italian in many ways but it's comforting and homely, which I think are the fundamentals of all Italian cooking.

INGREDIENTS

500g beef mince	500ml beef stock
500g pork mince	2 400ml tin chopped tomatoes
2 large onions, roughly chopped	2 tbsp gravy granules
1 stick of celery	1 tbsp Dijon mustard
2 carrots, no need to peel	1 tsp Wooster sauce
2 cloves garlic, minced	2 bay leaves
2 sprigs fresh rosemary	1 pack of lasagne sheets
White sauce (your favourite recipe).	50g grated cheddar

INSTRUCTIONS

Pop your onion, garlic, celery and carrot into a food processor and process until finely chopped.

Then add to a deep pan that's been heated with a little olive oil and salt and cook for about 5 minutes, stirring occasionally.

Once the onions are soft, add your beef and pork mince and brown all over, on a medium heat.

Add the chopped tomatoes, stock, mustard, Worcester sauce, bay leaves and rosemary, stir and bring to a boil.

Reduce to a simmer and simmer away for about an hour.

After an hour, add the gravy granules to add that extra beefy flavour and also thicken your sauce.

At this point taste for seasoning and add more salt and pepper if you think it needs more oomph.

Pop a layer of the meat sauce on the bottom of an oven proof dish, cover with a layer of lasagne sheets and finally a layer of white sauce.

Repeat this until you run out of meat sauce. You will likely have enough for about 3 layers.

Top with the cheddar and bake in a 180 fan pre-heated oven for about 30 minutes, until the top is brown and the lasagne is bubbling.

All that's left is to dig in and prepare for that food coma.

Brighter Days Ahead !

Whether it's the fact the sun's out, you have just got engaged, have a baby on the way or simply have just had a good week at work, these are all moments in life when we feel like the world is our oyster and we can do anything.

You feel at peace with yourself; life generally just feels good, and you feel like anything is possible.

In these moments, you are abundant with energy. You have forgone the need for afternoon naps, hiding away under a duvet and generally just wanting to be alone.

You want to be around people, you want to entertain and you want to show off your cooking skills with your nearest and dearest.

That's where this next section of the book comes in. It is full of a variety of recipes, some quick and simple, some low and slow, but all give that pizazz to your table that matches your mood.

These recipes are perfect for big family gatherings in the garden, last-minute friends over for wine or just a simple supper at home with your partner. We have got all bases covered and everyone who comes into contact with you, will not only be captivated by your radiance but also transfixed by the food you are delivering.

At these points in your life, you are on fire and nothing can stop you, so cook recipes that show off this mood in the most delicious way .

The Sun's Arrived, Picnic Time: You Can't Have A Picnic Without A Sausage Roll

SERVES: 20 sausage rolls PREP TIME: 5 MINUTES COOK TIME: 25 MINUTES

What is it about sausage rolls that make us think of summer day picnics but also that we just can't resist?

I am convinced that Greggs plant a chip in us after our first mouth-watering experience of their delectable, yet cost efficient, sausage rolls. This chip to be fired upon whenever sales are down and we are in our greatest need for the undeniable comfort that follows that first bite.

Clever strategy to be honest, and one I am fully on board with, but whatever it is, sausage rolls are a fundamental part of British culture.

They can be enjoyed at any time. On the sofa watching a film, in a pub with a beer, at your desk working away but they are never so right than on a hot summer's day, bathing in all its glory in some glorious London park. Pulled out of a lightly chilled Tupperware box and accompanied with something very pale and crisp in a glass.

My version are slightly different as they use filo instead of puff pastry. That's for two reasons really…

Firstly, because it's healthier and we all need that when we are going to get our summer bodies out. Secondly, it's that incredible crunch when you bite into them. A crunch you only get from filo pastry.

I hope you enjoy these as much as I do and I challenge you to only have one, it's something I have never been able to achieve.

INGREDIENTS

- 500g sausage meat
- 6 sheets filo pastry
- 1 tsp fresh thyme
- 1 tsp fennel seeds
- 50g melted butter
- Salt and pepper

INSTRUCTIONS

Mix together the sausage meat, thyme, fennel seeds, salt and pepper until well combined.

Lay a sheet of pastry flat and brush with butter. Top this layer of pastry with another and brush with more butter.

Spread the sausage mixture in a log shape across the longer side of the pastry and roll up into a long sausage roll.

Repeat this two more times and brush the top with a little melted butter.

Cut into small sausage rolls or keep them as they are if you would prefer a longer version.

Bake in the oven at 190 degrees Celsius (fan) for 25 minutes. They are ready when they are crisp and golden and the sausage meat is no longer pink!

Feeling Adventurous: Got To Be My Fish Pie With A Twist

SERVES: 4 PREP TIME: 5 MINUTES COOK TIME: 30 MINUTES

We all have those days when we are feeling adventurous and like we can take on the world. Maybe you have had an exceptionally good day at work, your kid has just won an award at school, you aced your Tough Mudder at the weekend, or maybe you just woke up without snoozing your alarm for the 15th time this morning.

Whatever the reason, you should capitalize on it, and even more so in the kitchen, by cooking something you wouldn't usually cook, not because it's complicated or involves hours in the kitchen but because it's just different.

A different ingredient, a different cuisine, the list goes on.

For me, fish pie is this exact meal. It's not something I would usually order in a restaurant, rarely cook at home and rarely think about when I am looking for cooking inspiration.

That's strange as I love fish and whenever I do have it or make it, I absolutely adore it.

It's one of life's unfathomable things, there is no rhyme or reason to it but it's just not my first choice.

When I do make it, I make a bit of a song and dance about it and it's usually for my other half when I either want to show him how much I love him or I have done something to annoy him. By replacing the mash with a sliced potato topping, you get a completely different texture.

Not that I am not a mash lover. Growing up in England, you can't help but love mash, but the crispy caramelised edges of a sliced potato topping just take this dish to a whole other level.

All you need alongside is a chilled glass of savvy B and some green beans, and maybe a few candles if you are feeling romantic.

INGREDIENTS

180g frozen prawns (defrosted)	300ml crème fraiche
1 banana shallot, finely chopped	6 medium potatoes, cut into rounds
2 cloves garlic, finely chopped	100ml milk
100g spinach	20g butter
Juice of 1/2 a lemon	Salt and pepper
Olive oil	

INSTRUCTIONS

Heat some olive oil in a large frying pan, over a medium heat and add your shallots and garlic. Cook this until your shallots are beautifully see through.

Add your prawns and cook for no more than a minute on each side, these will continue to cook in the oven so important not to overcook them at this stage.

Transfer the prawns to a plate for later but leave the shallots and garlic in the pan.

Pop in the crème fraiche and lemon juice and heat until completely melted, then add your milk and bring to a simmer.

Once your milky mixture is simmering, throw in your silky green spinach and cook for a few minutes until wilted.

Transfer this glutinous-looking but deceivingly healthy, creamy mixture to a baking dish along with your prawns.

Top the sauce with your sliced potatoes, arranging to cover the surface and brush with the melted butter before popping in a 180 degrees (fan) oven for around 30 minutes.

The pie is done when the sauce is bubbling and the potatoes have crisped up. Green beans are a great addition to this meal for added crunch!

The Humble Chickpea Can Be A Glorious Thing

SERVES: 4 PREP TIME: 10 MINUTES COOK TIME: 10 MINUTES

This is a recipe for those days when the sun is shining, you have had that perfect 8hrs of sleep and you are feeling great.

The sun may be shining but it's not quite got to that 30+ heat wave, however you know it's coming and you want to look desirable when you whip that shirt off.

This is the recipe for you and the best part is that you won't even feel like you're being healthy, whilst you're one step closer to that svelte body.

Chickpeas are an ingredient I came to later in life. If I am being honest, when I was younger, I was much more a burger and chips kind of guy, along with the many fad diets that were floating around in the early 2000s.

I didn't know what I was missing. When I discovered what flavour absorbers these small nuggets were, I never looked back.

By nature, the humble chickpea is very bland and requires punchy flavours, which is where this recipe is perfectly placed.

The vivacious mixture of red onion, creamy (yet light) mayo and punchy mustard and tuna are the perfect complements to this humblest of ingredients.

INGREDIENTS

1 can of tuna, drained	1 tbsp caper, roughly chopped
1 can chickpeas, drained	½ lemon, juiced
1 small red onion, roughly chopped	Handful fresh parsley, roughly chopped
2 tbsp low fat mayonnaise	90g wild rocket
1 tsp Dijon mustard	1 tbsp olive oil
½ tsp smoked paprika	Salt and pepper

INSTRUCTIONS

Grab your most visually appealing salad bowl, this salad is so simple but the flavours deserve to be served in something fit for company.

First make the dressing! Add your mayonnaise, Dijon mustard, capers, lemon juice, olive oil and a scatter of salt and pepper and mix it all together in your salad bowl.

Throw in the rest of the ingredients, apart from the smoked paprika, and mix well.

Now all that's left to do is sprinkle over the smoked paprika, dig in and enjoy how light you will feel after this ever-so-healthy meal. Best of all, you won't even feel like you're being healthy.

A Healthy Take On An Indian Takeaway Classic

SERVES: 4 PREP TIME: 15 MINUTES COOK TIME: 30 MINUTES

Like most English guys, particularly those born in the 90s, I have a nostalgic obsession with Indian food.

I say Indian food; no self-respecting Indian person could describe a korma as authentic, but it evokes happy memories of my childhood and teenage years and my first step into the world of Asian cooking.

My tastebuds have become a little more sophisticated since then, but a korma is still a firm favourite in the Bailey household.

This recipe is perfect for those days when you want the delicately mild, creaminess of a classic korma, but without the guilt that comes from having something so delicious that surely can't be good for you.

The minimal effort this takes and the simple ingredients mean it is a doddle and can be made on those days when you have no inclination to be in the kitchen.

It is even perfect to be dressed up for company, so it's a winner all round.

INGREDIENTS

- 1 onion, roughly chopped
- 2 fat cloves of garlic, roughly chopped
- 1 carrot, finely chopped
- 100g cashew nuts
- 1 400g tinned chopped tomatoes
- 50g coconut cream
- 1 250g packet of halloumi
- 1 tsp garam masala
- 1 tsp mild curry powder
- 1 tsp smoked paprika
- 1 tsp ground cumin
- Olive oil
- Salt and pepper
- 400g can of chickpeas

INSTRUCTIONS

Soak the cashews in some cold water whilst you cook your onions, garlic, carrot and a pinch of salt, in a little oil and over a medium heat.

Stirring occasionally for 10 minutes.

Add your dried spices and cook for a further 5 minutes.

Throw in your chopped tomatoes, some more salt, give everything a stir and simmer for another 15 minutes. Meanwhile, chop your halloumi into cubes and pop into the air fryer for about 6 minutes at 200, until nicely crispy.

Add your soaked cashews to the sauce, along with 250ml cold water, coconut cream and give everything a stir.

Blitz the sauce in a food processor or with a hand blender until smooth and thick.

Pop the sauce back into the pan over a low heat, along with your chickpeas and halloumi. Heat the chickpeas for about 2 minutes.

You're all done and all you need to do is enjoy with your favourite rice or flatbread. I just did some brown rice!

Get Togethers

We all love a get together with friends and family. For me, it's my real happy place when I have a great bunch of people around the table.

The laughter, storytelling, even the occasional bickering that you can only do with your nearest and dearest is a real thing of joy.

Regardless of this though, it can still be a daunting experience for the cook and especially in this time strapped world we live in where we seem to have less and less time for anything. The thought of cooking for a crowd can send you into hide on the sofa panic.

There are also those times when you have guests or children's friends pop round last minute and you have no idea what to cook for them.

But fear not, these recipes will show you that it cannot only be super simple but also enjoyable to cook for a crowd. Whatever the crowd may be.

From big dishes to plonk in the middle of the table and let the hungry hordes devour, to that fussy friend of your kids. There is something for everyone here and no one will go home disappointed, least of all the cook.

All you have to do is prepare yourself for all the compliments on your gastronomic talents and try not to blush.

My Kid's Fussy Friend: No One Can Resist Cream Cheese, Bacon And Pasta

SERVES: 4 PREP TIME: 5 MINUTES COOK TIME: 15 MINUTES

Kids always have those friends that you dread coming over. Not because they are precocious or obnoxious, but simply because they are such fussy eaters.

You could suck it up and think it's only one night, their parents have to deal with this every night. But you have enough to deal with, you don't need to be dealing with cooking two dinners as well.

That also interrupts your much deserved 20 minutes with your friends before chaos ensues.

The good news is, there is a recipe that even the fussiest dinosaur nugget eating child will not be able to turn their nose up to and, after all, you don't want to disappoint your little one by saying their best friend can't come over for dinner, so it's got to be worth a shot.

This low effort, high flavour explosion has never failed me. It's my bacon and cream cheese pasta.

Think carbonara but far less time consuming or pretentious to those little ears and what kid can resist bacon and cheese.

For that matter, what adult could?

Hope it works on little Jimmy's fussy friend.

INGREDIENTS

400g cups penne pasta (any pasta)	250g low fat cream cheese
2 rashers of bacon (any you have)	50g grated parmesan
2 cloves garlic, finely chopped	Salt and pepper

INSTRUCTIONS

Fry the bacon in a non-stick pan with no oil until cooked. The bacon will let off enough oil, so you don't need to add extra.

Remove the bacon and add the garlic to the bacon juices. Cook for a few minutes on a medium heat until the garlic is soft, be careful not to burn it.

Scoop in the cream cheese and sprinkle over the Parmesan. Reduce the heat to low and cook until it becomes thick, about 2 minutes.

Whilst the sauce is cooking, pop the pasta into boiling salted water and cook according to the package instructions.

When the pasta is cooked, drain it and reserve about 1/2 a cup of the cooking water.

Chop the bacon and add it, along with the pasta to the sauce. Stir to combine and if the sauce is struggling to coat the pasta add some of the pasta cooking water and that will help things along nicely!

Finally season with salt and pepper to taste.

You can add more Parmesan than the amount I have specified. I like to layer it on top.

Garlic spinach also goes great with this if you have some spinach and garlic knocking around.

Feeling Confident And Flirtatious: Revive The Beef Stew

SERVES: 6 PREP TIME: 5 MINUTES COOK TIME: 40 MINUTES

Feeling flirty, romantic and a little bit manly…

Maybe it's the first time the new special someone you have been seeing is coming over to your place and you want to impress them, maybe you looked in the mirror and did a big phwoar because you look so great at the moment or maybe you're having some friends over for dinner and that single special someone you like is one of the guests.

Whatever it is, don't just serve them your bog-standard beef stew. Not that there is anything bog standard about a beef stew. I, for one, love a stew, but it's not for you when you're in this mood. It needs to be elevated.

What better way to elevate it than by adding the glorious addition of velvety, crisp and buttery puff pastry. By simply whacking your leftover beef stew in a pie dish and topping it with pastry, you will elevate this most delicious of leftovers to a whole new level and people will think you have spent hours in the kitchen.

I know what you're thinking, isn't this a bit messy to eat in front of the absolute hottie you have invited or why on earth would I want to smell like garlic.

Guess what? The hottie is going to be as messy as you and if you are lucky enough to get a goodbye kiss, you will both taste of garlic anyway, so relax and enjoy.

INGREDIENTS

Leftover beef stew, about 500g	1 egg
1 sheet of ready rolled puff pastry	1 tsp milk

INSTRUCTIONS

Preheat the oven to 180 degrees Celsius.

Transfer your cold leftover beef stew to a large baking dish. You want the stew to be fairly thick so if there's too much liquid, add 1 tbsp gravy granules and it will thicken up nicely when it heats.

Top with your ready rolled puff pastry, beat your egg with your milk and brush all over the top of your puff pastry. Cut a hole in the middle of the puff pastry and pop in the oven for 30 to 40 minutes, until the stew is bubbling and the pastry is golden brown.

All you need with this is green beans or if you are feeling really naughty, chips.

Never Happier Than When The Family Is Home: Pasta Is The Only Way To Go

SERVES: 4 PREP TIME: 5 MINUTES COOK TIME: 50 MINUTES

Nowadays, we lead such busy lives and with the ease of air travel, families are living further and further apart from each other.

A blessing and a curse of this instant gratification society that we live in. When we are all together, particularly in my family, it is even more special.

All families are different but when mine get together, there is generally a lot of wine being consumed and a lot of laughter.

Like every family, there is the matriarch. This was once my dearly departed Nan, but it is now my aunty. She always puts on a good spread, making it look so effortless and easy with my uncle.

When I think of family get-togethers, I think of that big dish in the middle of the table and everyone taking hearty portions of whatever delicious morsel is in it.

This is where this recipe came from….

It had been a busy week, and I had my mum's side of the family over. Very unlike me, I hadn't planned the event very well and had wanted to make my stuffed pasta shells, but forgot to buy the vital ingredient, large pasta shells.

By the way, they are incredibly hard to find in Hertfordshire, it appears.

Did I give up? Did I fall to the floor in a strop like a child in the supermarket? No. I put my big boy pants on and adapted the recipe with whatever pasta I had in the cupboard.

No one noticed and everyone loved it, so it is now a firm family favourite.

INGREDIENTS

2 400ml tinned tomatoes	250g ricotta
2 large cloves garlic, finely chopped	250g spinach, cooked & chopped
1 large onion, finely chopped	1 tbsp tomato puree
250g any pasta	50g grated parmesan
1 tbsp dried oregano	Olive oil
¼ tsp dried chili flakes	Salt and pepper
1 tbsp honey	Handful fresh basil, roughly chopped
250g mascarpone	¼ tsp ground nutmeg

INSTRUCTIONS

Heat some oil in a shallow casserole dish and add your onion, along with a little salt and cook for about 5 minutes. The onion is done when they become translucent and they start to smell like those fried onions you get on top of deliciously processed van burgers.

Add the garlic, oregano, chili flakes and tomato puree and cook for a few minutes, to release the flavours.

Add your tinned tomatoes, along with a little salt and pepper and the honey. Give it a stir and bring to the boil.

Add about 1/2 cup water and reduce the heat to a simmer and simmer gently for about 30 minutes, adding more water if it gets too dry.

Whilst the tomatoes are cooking, make your mascarpone mix.

Mix together the mascarpone, ricotta, chopped spinach and nutmeg in a bowl and dollop tablespoon blobs on top of the tomato mixture.

Top the dish with grated Parmesan and place in the oven at 180 degrees for about 20 minutes, until bubbly and brown.

Whilst the sauce is cooking, boil your pasta according to the packet instructions and set aside. Once the sauce is ready, remove from the oven and dish up.

Serve some pasta in a bowl and top with a generous helping of the sauce and mascarpone mixture, followed by a sprinkle of fresh basil.

Unexpected Guests: A Mediterranean Marvel

SERVES: 4 PREP TIME: 5 MINUTES COOK TIME: 25 MINUTES

We have all been there when those unexpected guests arrive around teatime and you have that overwhelming sense of: "What on earth am I going to feed these people?"

The answer to this question generally depends on who has popped round unexpectedly. Is it your best friend, last minute play date, in-laws? The list goes on and on, and no matter how much they say, "Oh, don't worry. We are fine," we all know they don't mean it.

This recipe may not be for all these unexpected guests, but it sure will impress most of them. Not only that, but they will also think you are an absolute legend as it looks far more complicated than it actually is.

The first time I tried this fish stew, I was a typical 22-year-old English guy, who thought that fish was always covered in batter and eaten on a Friday.

It never occurred to me you could stew fish, not deep fry it, and it would be delicious.

I was incredibly wrong. Just the smell alone takes me back to the basil infused hills of the Liguria Coast. It takes me back to a time of no responsibilities, of peace and of moments of finding yourself.

Enough of my telenovella dramatics. To sum up, it was a great time and this recipe is an absolute must for those unexpected guests.

INGREDIENTS

3 frozen cod fillets	Handful of fresh basil and parsley, roughly chopped
170g frozen prawns	1 tbsp dried oregano
1 yellow onion, roughly chopped	¼ tsp crushed chili flakes
3 cloves garlic, finely chopped	Zest of a whole lemon, juice of half
350g passata	Olive oil
500ml fish stock	Salt and pepper

INSTRUCTIONS

Heat some oil in a large saucepan over a medium heat and cook the onion until soft for about 5 minutes, stirring occasionally.

Add the garlic, oregano, chili flakes, a little salt and pepper and cook for 2 minutes to soften the garlic and let everything blend together.

Now pour in the passata and fish stock, bring to the boil, reduce the heat to medium and simmer for 10 minutes.

By this time, the kitchen will smell exceptional.

Drop in the frozen cod and cook for 10 minutes, then add the frozen prawns. Cook for a further 3 minutes until the prawns turn a lovely pale pink colour.

By this point, the prawns will be cooked and the cod will be nice and flaky.

Finally squeeze in the juice of your lemon and the zest, followed by the fresh herbs and stir together with a little salt and pepper before digging in.

Enjoy this delicious stew with any bread of your liking, but an olive loaf is exceptional with this dish!

Left The Boxing Day Party To The Last Minute: Turkey Pie Is The Answer

SERVES: 6 PREP TIME: 15 MINUTES COOK TIME: 30 MINUTES

I don't care what anyone says we are all guilty of this one. You have gotten through Christmas and are feeling slightly jaded after your bad influence relative poured you that one glass of port too many.

But now it's Boxing Day and you have more relatives arriving, because you come from a broken home you feel like you spend the whole Christmas period entertaining one strand of the family after another. But it's the festive period and you secretly love being the host/hostess with the mostess.

Now don't get me wrong you knew they were coming, but you put it to the back of your mind and thought it's ok we will figure it out on the day. But now the day has arrived and the sense of panic and dread that isn't totally due to the hangover has taken over your body.

But I'm here to tell you not to worry. You will have leftover turkey, potatoes, veg and more than likely some sort of cream or crème fraîche lurking in the fridge.

So you have everything you need for a velvety rich and creamy turkey pie. Just what you need to feed the horde and cure that delicate head, well that and a few glasses of fizz.

INGREDIENTS

Leftover turkey, about 500g (any part)	100g butter (approximately)
2 cloves garlic, finely chopped	Crème fraiche or double cream (whatever you have left)
1 rashers of bacon, roughly chopped	Grated parmesan
500ml turkey or chicken stock	Any fresh herbs you have (optional)
2 tbsp plain flour	Olive oil
500g potatoes, peeled and roughly chopped	Salt and pepper

INSTRUCTIONS

Fry the bacon in a little olive oil until crisp, then add the garlic for a few minutes. Once your kitchen smells like the streets of Florence the garlic is cooked enough.

Remove the bacon and garlic to a separate plate. Add a generous knob of butter (about 2tbsp) and the flour, stir for a few minutes to cook out the flour.

Slowly add the stock, whisking as you go to avoid lumps. Once all the stock is added, bubble away for a few minutes until the desired thickness. Season to taste.

Add the bacon, garlic and leftover turkey to the sauce and stir to combine. You can add a few dollops of cream or crème fraiche at this stage, if you have it and want that oh so delectable creaminess.

Leave to cool, whilst you get on with the potato topping.

Boil your peeled and chopped potatoes in salted water until tender and then mash with enough butter to make them smooth. Remember to add salt and pepper here to season too, otherwise your mash will be bland. Always taste your mash too, making sure you have enough butter and seasoning.

Pour the cooled turkey mixture into an oven proof dish and top with the mash potato, smoothing with a spatula.

Top with grated Parmesan or any cheese you have left over and bake for around 30 minutes in a 180 Celsius (fan) oven. If you would like the top crispier, just pop it under the grill for a few minutes after the previous step.

Indulge Your Inner Popeye And Embrace That Warm Feeling: Greek Spanakopita

SERVES: 6 PREP TIME: 10 MINUTES COOK TIME: 30 MINUTES

Greece is not a place I usually go to for recipe inspiration and not for any prejudice you understand, it's just not a cuisine I have been overly exposed too.

Oh, what a shame that is though. The cuisine and culture are incredibly similar to my beloved Italy, the same hedonistic way of being and the same passion for food.

Spanakopita is a dish I have had on and off over the years, usually from those wonderful farmers markets dotted around the UK. But I never thought to attempt to make it.

This dish always seemed so complicated and complex, at least that's how it seemed from the flavours. But if there is anything I have learnt is big flavour doesn't have to mean complicated.

One thing is for sure this dish is perfect for those bright times of the year. It's light and flaky texture are perfect for picnics, light lunches and any other time of the day.

INGREDIENTS

4 slices filo pastry

150g feta cheese

180g sun dried tomatoes, roughly chopped

olive oil

200g spinach

2 medium eggs

Pepper to season

INSTRUCTIONS

Preheat your oven to 160 fan and prepare your spinach by wilting it down over a medium heat in a pan with some olive oil. Keep stirring it around and it will wilt in seconds.

Transfer this to a sieve and leave to cool & drain off excess the liquid. You want to remove as much water as possible from the spinach.

In a bowl, mix together your chopped sun-dried tomatoes, crumble in the feta, chopped spinach, before finally adding your eggs and mixing well to combine.

Lay a sheet of filo on a chopping board and brush with the sun dried tomato oil all over. Lay brushed side down in a loose bottom cake tin, making sure it overlaps over one side for the top.

Repeat with the remaining filo, layering around the tin and over lapping so you have four healthy layers, then tip your filling in and distribute well.

Fold over the edges of the filo to cover the top and give the top a final brush with some sun dried tomato oil, before popping in the oven for 30 minutes.